NATIONAL GEOGRAPHIC | GLOBAL ISSUES

WATER RESOURCES

D1302438

Andrew J. Milson, Ph.D.
Content Consultant
University of Texas at Arlington

Acknowledgments

Grateful acknowledgment is given to the authors, artists, photographers, museums, publishers, and agents for permission to reprint copyrighted material. Every effort has been made to secure the appropriate permission. If any omissions have been made or if corrections are required, please contact the Publisher.

Instructional Consultant: Christopher Johnson, Evanston, Illinois

Teacher Reviewer: Linda O'Connor, Northeast Independent School District, San Antonio, Texas

Photographic Credits

Cover, Inside Front Cover, Title Page ©Hardi Budi/ National Geographic Stock. **3** (bg) ©Gary Nolton/ Getty Images. **4** (bg) ©Laurent Piechegut/Bios/ photolibrary.com. **6** (bg) ©Thomas Wolke-UNEP/Still Pictures/photolibrary.com. (cl) ©Dr. Gopal Murti/ Photo Researchers, Inc. **7** (tr) ©Joel Sartore/National Geographic Stock. **8** (bg) Mapping Specialists. **10** (bg) ©AP Photo/Juan Karita. **11** (bl) ©REUTERS/ David Mercado. **12** (t) ©Krystian Bielatowicz/Visavis. pl/Aurora Photos. **13** (br) ©Justus de Cuveland/ imagebroker/Alamy. **14** (bg) ©Escudero Patrick/ Hemis/Alamy. **15** (tl) ©Juan Karita/AP Photo. **16** (bg) ©REUTERS/Chor Sokunthea. (bl) ©Barbara Walton/epa/Corbis. **19** (bg) ©Angela Prati/age footstock. (tl) ©Mario Weigt/Anzenberger/Redux. **20** (br) ©TANG CHHIN SOTHY/AFP/Getty Images. **21** (bg) ©REUTERS/Chor Sokunthea. **22** (bg) ©Joel Sartore/National Geographic Stock. **24** (c) NASA Goddard Space Flight Center (http://visibleearth.nasa. gov/). **25** (bg) ©Kip Evans Photography. **27** (t) ©Mark Dye/Star Ledger/Corbis. **28** (tr) ©Fred Hirschmann/ Science Faction/Corbis. **30** (br) ©Dr. Gopal Murti/ Photo Researchers, Inc. (tr) ©Eric PHAN-KIM/Flickr/ Getty Images. **31** (bl) ©Chris Harris/All Canada Photos/agefotostock. (br) ©Kip Evans Photography. (tr) ©Laurent Piechegut/Bios/photolibrary.com. (bg) ©Gary Nolton/Getty Images.

For permission to use material from this text or product, submit all requests online at www.cengage.com/permissions.

Further permissions questions can be emailed to permissionrequest@cengage.com.

Visit National Geographic Learning online at www.NGSP.com.

Visit our corporate website at www.cengage.com.

Printed in the USA.

RR Donnelley, Jefferson City, MO

ISBN: 978-07362-97493

12 13 14 15 16 17 18 19 20 21

10 9 8 7 6 5 4 3 2 1

WATER
WO

HOW IS POLLUTION THREATENING WATER QUALITY AROUND THE WORLD?

Water covers two-thirds of Earth's surface. As a result, we do not have to worry about wasting it, right? Wrong! About 97 percent of the world's water is saline, or salty. That means that only about 3 percent is good for drinking and growing crops. Two percent of this freshwater is frozen in polar ice or trapped in underground rock layers called **aquifers**. Yet even freshwater cannot be used if it is polluted. If we want to preserve what little water we have, we have to keep it clean.

WHERE WATER IS FOUND ON EARTH

Oceans
96.5%

Freshwater
3.5%

Source: U.S. Geological Survey

DIRTY WATER

Pollutants are substances that make the environment and our water dirty. Drinking these substances can make people very sick. About 3.3 million people die from drinking polluted water every year. Most are children under the age of five.

Sometimes water pollutants come from natural sources, such as rotting plant material. Natural disasters, such as earthquakes, floods, hurricanes, and tsunamis, can also damage water sources. These disasters can wash large amounts of waste into the water.

Animal and human waste can make water dirty too. Without good sewage treatment, this waste can carry bacteria into water supplies. **Bacteria** are one-celled organisms that can cause diseases. In developing countries, diseases caused by polluted water make up four-fifths of all illnesses.

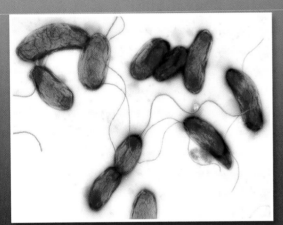

This bacteria carries cholera, a disease caused by drinking dirty water.

If not disposed of correctly, almost everything we throw away can end up in the sea—including rusty old bicycles.

HUMAN ACTIONS

Other sources of pollution are human-made. Chemicals, including pesticides and fertilizers, are among the largest sources of pollution. Scientists say that the world's water supplies contain more than a million different chemicals.

Pollution also comes from burning **fossil fuels**, such as coal and oil. These energy sources are formed by the fossilized remains of plants and animals that have been buried in the earth for millions of years. When coal and oil are burned for energy, gases are released. These gases mix with water vapor in the air. This vapor condenses and falls to Earth as acid rain. Acid rain pollutes lakes, streams, and rivers. Accidents that occur when companies drill for oil can also damage our waters. An oil spill at sea can damage sea life, beaches, and birds.

It may take years to undo the damage to wildlife caused by the 2010 Gulf of Mexico oil spill.

Developing countries that do not have clean water and good sanitation have high rates of disease, poverty, and hunger. Many of these countries have found ways to clean their polluted water.

In the following pages, you will read about two places—South America's Lake Titicaca and Southeast Asia's Mekong River—with serious water pollution problems. People in both places are learning how to clean up their water. Their efforts show that we can do something about water pollution.

Explore the Issue

1. **Summarize** What are some of the sources of water pollution?

2. **Analyze Cause and Effect** What impact does water pollution have on humans?

WORLD Hot Spots
Industrial Wate

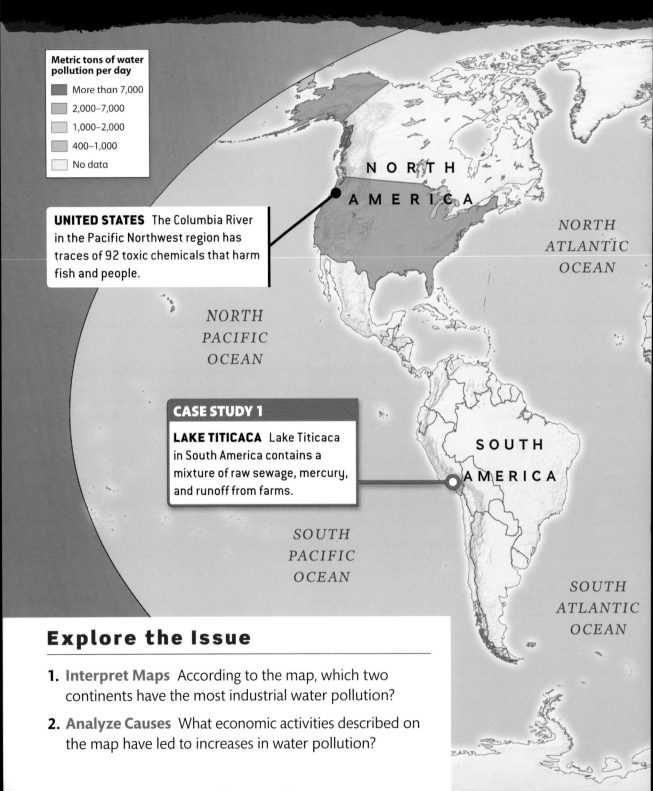

Metric tons of water pollution per day

- More than 7,000
- 2,000–7,000
- 1,000–2,000
- 400–1,000
- No data

NORTH AMERICA

NORTH ATLANTIC OCEAN

UNITED STATES The Columbia River in the Pacific Northwest region has traces of 92 toxic chemicals that harm fish and people.

NORTH PACIFIC OCEAN

CASE STUDY 1

LAKE TITICACA Lake Titicaca in South America contains a mixture of raw sewage, mercury, and runoff from farms.

SOUTH AMERICA

SOUTH PACIFIC OCEAN

SOUTH ATLANTIC OCEAN

Explore the Issue

1. **Interpret Maps** According to the map, which two continents have the most industrial water pollution?

2. **Analyze Causes** What economic activities described on the map have led to increases in water pollution?

Pollution

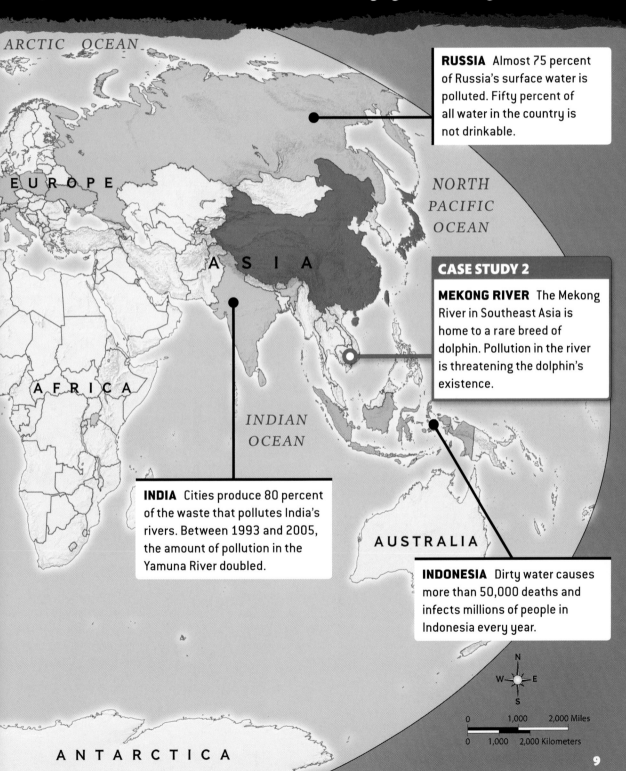

ARCTIC OCEAN

RUSSIA Almost 75 percent of Russia's surface water is polluted. Fifty percent of all water in the country is not drinkable.

EUROPE

NORTH PACIFIC OCEAN

ASIA

CASE STUDY 2

MEKONG RIVER The Mekong River in Southeast Asia is home to a rare breed of dolphin. Pollution in the river is threatening the dolphin's existence.

AFRICA

INDIAN OCEAN

INDIA Cities produce 80 percent of the waste that pollutes India's rivers. Between 1993 and 2005, the amount of pollution in the Yamuna River doubled.

AUSTRALIA

INDONESIA Dirty water causes more than 50,000 deaths and infects millions of people in Indonesia every year.

N
W E
S

| 0 | 1,000 | 2,000 Miles |
| 0 | 1,000 | 2,000 Kilometers |

ANTARCTICA

Young Peruvian boys try to clean up Lake Titicaca. The rapid growth of cities in the region has led to increased pollution in the lake.

Cleaning Up
LAKE
TITICACA

A NATURAL WONDER

The Inca civilization arose in Peru in the 1200s. The Inca people believed that the gods they worshipped had once sent a great flood to the area to put an end to evil. The people believed that when the flood waters dried, they left behind a large pool of dark blue water high in the Andes Mountains. The Inca called the pool Lake Titicaca. They considered the lake to be sacred and pure.

Lake Titicaca is an ancient lake. Experts believe that it has existed for three million years. Lake Titicaca is so old that the prehistoric saber-toothed tiger might have drunk water from the lake. In fact, the name *titicaca* may refer to a member of the cat family. The name could mean "rock of the puma" in the native language of the Andean people. Whatever the name means, Lake Titicaca is considered to be one of the world's great natural wonders.

A LAKE AT RISK

Lake Titicaca lies on the border between Bolivia and Peru. However, Titicaca is an important lake for all of South America. It is the continent's largest source of freshwater. It is also home to many unusual plant and animal species, including a huge water frog that is found nowhere else. In addition, Lake Titicaca is the world's highest lake that is also **navigable**. That means that boats or ships can sail on the lake.

Unfortunately, Lake Titicaca has become badly polluted. Today the lake contains a **toxic**, or poisonous, mix of raw sewage, industrial waste, and agricultural runoff. Bad smells rise from parts of the lake, and dead fish float on its surface. Many people are now afraid to drink the lake's water or let their animals drink it. If water pollution destroys Lake Titicaca, all South Americans will feel the loss.

A Peruvian woman collects water from Lake Titicaca. Some people who live along its polluted shores only use the water to wash their clothes.

People on Lake Titicaca try to steer their boats through thick weeds known as water lentils.

A VARIETY OF POLLUTANTS

The pollution of Lake Titicaca began at least 50 years ago. A number of activities has contributed to the lake's decline during this time. People in cities and towns have dumped their untreated human and animal waste into the lake. Over the same period, agriculture and ranching expanded in the region. Manure and fertilizer runoff from these farms and fields washed into local rivers. The rivers then carried that pollution into Lake Titicaca.

Mining activities have also harmed the lake. Officials estimate that as many as 30,000 small mines operate along rivers that feed into Lake Titicaca. Many of these mines are illegal and do not obey the rules for cleaning up. They dump toxic chemicals and other materials into the water. In addition, water removal and droughts have added to the lake's troubles by reducing water levels. As these levels decrease, the concentration of pollution in the water increases.

THE WATER LENTIL INVASION

The polluted waters of Lake Titicaca have attracted a species of weed called water lentils, which float on the surface of the water and turn it bright green. The lentils grow in parts of the lake and form a thick mat that is hard to break up. They also absorb much of the oxygen in the water. As a result, some of the fish in Lake Titicaca are **suffocating**, or dying from lack of oxygen. Local groups have tried using giant strainers to scoop up the lentils, but the lentils grow back. To get rid of them, the polluted mud at the bottom of the lake must also be removed. Removal is difficult, however, because the lake contains about 800,000 tons of this mud.

When fish die, other forms of wildlife suffer too. Many plants and animals live in and around Lake Titicaca. It also provides shelter for migrating birds. However, the birds may stop returning to a lake that is full of dead fish.

A frog pokes its head out of a mat of water lentils. Waste dumped in Lake Titicaca has encouraged the growth of the weeds.

13

The water around the Island of the Sun, one of Lake Titicaca's largest islands, is free from pollution. South Americans hope that one day the rest of Lake Titicaca will be just as clean.

JOINING FORCES

As you have learned, Lake Titicaca lies between the border of Bolivia and Peru. For a time, the two countries had different ideas about caring for the lake. They could not even agree on how to measure the pollution. This lack of cooperation allowed the problem to get worse.

Today everyone agrees that a team effort is necessary to protect Lake Titicaca. As a result, Peru and Bolivia have joined forces on the issue. They have created a single organization with authority for preserving the lake. They have also worked to enforce environmental laws that will help to decrease pollution.

Men clean Lake Titicaca's Pajchiri Bay in Bolivia. Officials in Peru and Bolivia agreed to work together to clean the bay after high levels of arsenic were found in the water.

Other groups have also organized to help clean up the lake. They come from many different cities, schools, environmental groups, and government agencies. Even the United Nations has gotten involved. Money from these international groups has been used to build more sewers to carry waste away from Lake Titicaca. Plans for building more water treatment plants along the lake are also being developed.

Researchers from all these groups and organizations are now collecting and sharing information. Some are **monitoring**, or supervising, water quality around the lake. Others are using satellites to take pictures of the lake high above its waters. They are sharing data so everyone can work together. With cooperation and hard work, one of the oldest lakes on Earth has a bright future.

Explore the Issue

1. **Analyze Causes** What are three causes of pollution in Lake Titicaca?

2. **Identify Problems and Solutions** How are the governments of Bolivia and Peru teaming up to protect Lake Titicaca?

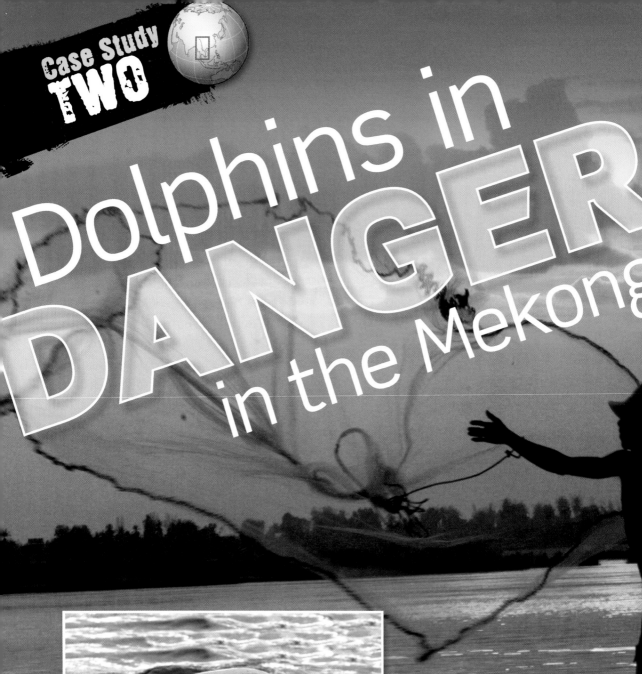

Dolphins in DANGER in the Mekong

In 2005, the total population of Irrawaddy dolphins was estimated at 127. Today, there may be as few as 86.

LIFE IN A COMPLEX RIVER

In Cambodia, the still surface of the Mekong River sparkles in the early morning light. The only sounds are twittering birds and rushing water. Suddenly, a sleek, gray head breaks the surface of the river. The head rises above the water and views its surroundings, while spitting a stream of water from its mouth. Then just as suddenly, the head dips and disappears beneath the water. An Irrawaddy dolphin has come and gone.

The Mekong is a long and complex river. It begins high in the Tibetan Plateau as snow melts to water and flows down some of the world's highest mountains. In China, the river cuts through **gorges**, or deep, narrow passages surrounded by steep canyon walls. The Mekong then flows through Myanmar, Laos, Thailand, Cambodia, and Vietnam. In all, the river travels over 2,600 miles before it empties out into the South China Sea. Along its course, the Mekong is home to more than 1,200 species of fish including seven species of giant fish, more than any other river. Among the world's rivers, the Mekong is one of the most **biodiverse**, or filled with different life-forms, in the world.

DISAPPEARING DOLPHINS

At the mouth of the Mekong River is a triangular deposit of soil and silt, or **delta**. This area is the Irrawaddy dolphins' home. Beautiful and shy, the dolphins slide through these warm, shallow waters, catching fish and playing. Many people along the Mekong consider the Irrawaddy dolphin sacred. Local people and visitors come to the river to see them. The dolphins are so popular that a tourist industry has developed around them. Unfortunately, the river dolphin is in great danger of extinction, or dying out.

The dolphin population in the Mekong River has been steadily decreasing for several years. Many newborns die within the first few weeks of life. As a result, when older dolphins die, they are not replaced. Experts believe that the newborn dolphins are dying as a result of human activity. The Mekong runs through heavily populated regions in six countries. People in these regions are changing how they work and live—and that is affecting the river and the Irrawaddy dolphins.

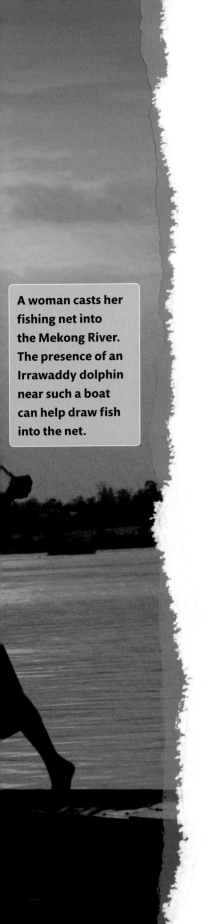

A woman casts her fishing net into the Mekong River. The presence of an Irrawaddy dolphin near such a boat can help draw fish into the net.

POPULATION IMPACT

The increase in population along the Mekong River is a result of **urbanization**, or the growth of large cities. Today more than 16 million people live along the Mekong Delta. As people have moved into the delta, some of the dolphins and other animals in the river have lost their **habitat**, or natural home. Much of this loss has occurred as dams have been built on the Mekong. The dams help capture water for use in the new industries that have developed in the delta. The water is also used to create energy supplies for the growing population. The animals in the river lose more of their habitat when people deforest the land and develop mines. These activities can change the river's flow, increase pollution levels, and turn the water murky with soil.

Agriculture causes further changes. Farmers are growing more food for the expanding population. The fertilizers and pesticides they use sometimes end up in the water. Plants and animals living in the river are harmed by these toxic chemicals.

FISH FARMING

Another activity that is harming the Mekong is aquaculture, or fish farming. Aquaculture is the practice of raising fish for food in tanks or pens rather than catching them in the sea. Aquaculture is booming because people continually demand more and more seafood. In the countries along the Mekong River, people eat more than twice as much fish as people in North America and Europe. However, aquaculture does not just satisfy the needs of local people. Fish farms represent the fastest-growing form of animal food production in the world. Some experts have estimated that fish farms produce half of all the fish eaten by humans today.

On the one hand, aquaculture is beneficial because it helps satisfy world hunger and decrease the practice of overfishing the oceans. On the other hand, aquaculture damages the environment because it can decrease the populations of wild fish and spread disease. It can also increase pollution. Fish farms, like agricultural farms, create a great deal of raw waste. This waste often ends up in streams, rivers, and oceans, where it pollutes the water and harms fish and other life-forms.

Some families in the Mekong Delta raise fish in cages under their floating houses. This Vietnamese girl is feeding her family's fish.

The Mekong Delta is known as the "rice bowl" of Vietnam. Like the farmers shown in this photo, about 80 percent of the country's population grows rice.

BACTERIAL DISEASES

Some practices that were once believed to threaten the Irrawaddy dolphins are no longer considered harmful. For example, at one time, researchers thought dolphins were dying as a result of boating accidents and getting caught in fishing nets. However, when researchers tested dead dolphins, they found high levels of chemical pollutants, such as mercury and pesticides, in their blood. In addition, researchers discovered that the Mekong Delta is contaminated with deadly bacteria. Some scientists think the bacteria are coming from fish farms along the river.

As a result of these findings, conservationists, or people who work to protect wildlife, now think the dolphins are dying from bacterial diseases. The dolphins are getting sick because water pollutants have weakened the animals' ability to fight the diseases.

NEW HOPE FOR IRRAWADDY DOLPHINS

There may not be much that can be done to save the Irrawaddy dolphins in the Mekong from extinction. However, scientists have learned valuable lessons from the dolphins' situation. They have learned about fishing practices that endanger dolphins. They have also found out what happens when an animal's natural habitat is destroyed. Finally, scientists have been able to study the effects of water pollution on wildlife.

Fortunately, there is still hope for Irrawaddy dolphins in other parts of the world. In 2009, a population of nearly 6,000 dolphins was discovered living off the coast of Bangladesh. The dolphins there are safe from the problems and pollution that people can bring—for now. Conservationists are working to make sure this group survives so that the Irrawaddy dolphin does not disappear forever.

River guards patrol the Mekong, on the lookout for illegal fishing practices. These practices may harm the Irrawaddy dolphins.

Explore the Issue

1. **Summarize** Why are the dolphins in the Mekong River Delta dying? Give two reasons.

2. **Draw Conclusions** The dolphins are dying in some places but doing well in others. What conclusions can you draw about those different environments?

Some groups have recommended introducing dolphin conservation zones to save the remaining Irrawaddy dolphins in the Mekong River.

Fortunately, there is still hope for Irrawaddy dolphins in other parts of the world.

Marine
Protected Areas
&
Water
Pollution

Smoke rises from the surface of the Gulf of Mexico as cleanup crews burn oil spilled in 2010.

GULF OIL SPILL

In November 2010, scientists diving in the Gulf of Mexico saw something disturbing on the ocean floor. Huge coral formations were dead or dying. They were also covered with a strange, thick black substance.

The scientists weren't sure what the black substance was. However, they believed it was oil. They guessed that it came from the gigantic spill caused when the Deepwater Horizon oil drilling platform exploded in April 2010. The explosion was an example of pollution caused by humans. In this case, the oil spill damaged one of the world's richest ecosystems.

For all their power, oceans are fragile. They give us food, oxygen, and predictable weather. In return, we give them trash, carbon dioxide, and runoff from farms. That's not a very fair trade. Now the oceans are showing the effects. In some of these waters, fish are disappearing, and all marine life is suffering.

S.O.S. = SAVE OUR SEAS

We need to protect our seas, and National Geographic is answering the call. The organization is now teaming with scientists concerned about ocean health. Two of those scientists are Sylvia Earle and Enric Sala, Explorers-in-Residence at National Geographic. Earle and Sala are working with government groups around the world to establish marine protected areas, or MPAs. **Marine protected areas** are regions in or near oceans where human activity is limited to preserve marine life.

Some MPAs work to restore fish populations in oceans. Others preserve a fragile ecosystem or historical site. Scientists are also using MPAs to research how healthy seas function. This research will help them learn how to preserve the seas.

Marine protected areas are one way people can fight the effects of pollution, overfishing, and habitat destruction. Overfishing occurs when fish are caught faster than they can be replaced by the marine population in a body of water. Of course, more efforts are needed, but MPAs are a good place to start.

RESTORING OUR OCEANS' HEALTH

Both Earle and Sala want to preserve our oceans. Earle is an **oceanographer**, or scientist who studies oceans and marine life. In 2010, the Sylvia Earle Alliance teamed with the National Geographic Society and the Waitt Foundation to found Mission Blue. Mission Blue is a global partnership that works to restore the oceans' health and productivity and create more MPAs.

Sala is a marine ecologist who grew up exploring the sea off Spain's coast. Today he heads the Pristine Seas project. The project works to find, study, and preserve healthy, untouched ocean sites. Sala is establishing MPAs in the Mediterranean Sea. He hopes to use the knowledge he gains from these MPAs to help restore damaged marine environments.

Our planet's health starts—or ends—with the state of the oceans' health. You can join National Geographic in making a positive difference. First, learn more about water pollution, overfishing, and climate change. Then get involved. The activity on the next two pages can help you get started.

HOPE SPOTS The dots on this map represent the MPAs—Hope Spots— that Earle has helped establish through Mission Blue.

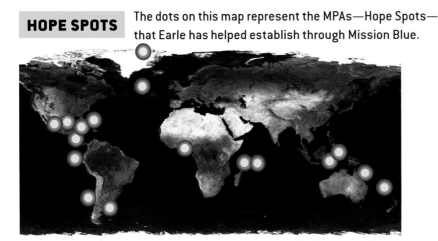

Explore the Issue

1. **Analyze Causes** What are three causes of pollution in the ocean?

2. **Explain** Why are Sylvia Earle and Enric Sala helping to establish marine protected areas?

"With every
breath we take,
every drop of
water we drink,
we're connected
to the ocean."
—Sylvia Earle

National Geographic Explorer-
in-Residence Sylvia Earle
explores the sea off the coast of
Honduras in Central America.

Rescue a River
—and report your results

You don't have to be a marine scientist to fight for our water sources. You just have to care—and get involved. One way to help is to identify a polluted river, lake, pond, or stream in your community and clean it up. With a little bit of work, you can make a big difference.

IDENTIFY

- Find out about the quality of the water sources in your community.

- Talk to experts at your local museum, university, or local water department to identify a body of water that needs help.

- Ask what steps you can take to clean up the water or improve it in other ways.

ORGANIZE

- Advertise in your school paper or place posters in your neighborhood to recruit volunteers.

- Gather the supplies you'll need to clean up: gloves, garbage bags, shovels, and water-testing kits.

- Identify an appropriate place to dispose of the garbage.

Volunteers pick up trash along the Rahway River in New Jersey.

DOCUMENT

- Take before-and-after photos of the site and perform before-and-after water tests to measure the results of your work. Have an adult help you take the tests and dispose of the water.

- List the pollutants you find and the strategies you use to deal with them.

- Videotape and interview the volunteers about their experiences.

SHARE

- Use your photos and videos to create a multimedia presentation of your cleanup effort and show it to your class.

- Describe your efforts—and the difference you made—in an article for your school or community paper.

- Inspire others to take up the battle by sharing your story and your ideas for reclaiming water sources in a talk at your local library.

Write an Informative Article

Lake Erie, which is one of the Great Lakes, was in terrible shape during the 1960s. However, in an amazing turnaround, much of Lake Erie is clean today, and fish and vegetation are thriving. How did people bring Lake Erie back to life? *That* is the topic you will research and write about.

RESEARCH

Use the Internet, books, and articles to research and answer the following questions:

- What condition was Lake Erie in during the 1960s?
- How had the lake become so polluted?
- How was the lake cleaned up?

As you carry out your research, be sure to take notes in your own words and keep a list of the sources you use.

DRAFT

Review your notes and then write a first draft.

- Introduce your topic—the pollution of Lake Erie—in the first paragraph. Organize your ideas using strategies such as cause and effect and chronological order.

- Develop your topic in the second paragraph with relevant facts from reliable sources to explain how people cleaned up Lake Erie. Use transitions and precise language and maintain a formal style.

- Provide a concluding section in the third paragraph to explain what the effects of the cleanup of Lake Erie have been.

REVISE & EDIT

Read your first draft to make sure that it gives solid information about the cleanup of Lake Erie.

- Does your first paragraph introduce your topic?

- Does the second paragraph develop your topic and clearly explain how people cleaned up Lake Erie?

- Have you described the effects of the cleanup effort in your conclusion in the third paragraph?

Use the above questions to revise the article. Then check your paper for errors in spelling and punctuation. Are names spelled correctly? Are quotations accurate? Be sure you have the information in a logical order.

PUBLISH & PRESENT

Now you are ready to publish and present your article. Add any images or graphs that will help illustrate or support your ideas. Then print out the article or write a clean copy by hand. Post the article in your classroom to share with the class.

Visual GLOSSARY

aquifer *n.*, an underground rock layer containing water

bacteria *n.*, one-celled organisms that can cause diseases

biodiverse *adj.*, filled with different life-forms

delta *n.*, a triangular deposit of soil and silt at the mouth of a river

fossil fuel *n.*, an energy source such as oil, coal, and natural gas, formed by the fossilized remains of plants and animals

gorge *n.*, a deep, narrow passage surrounded by steep canyon walls

habitat *n.*, the natural home of a living thing

marine protected area *n.*, a region in or near an ocean where human activity is limited in order to preserve marine life

monitor *v.*, to supervise

navigable *adj.*, deep and wide enough to allow boats or ships to sail on

oceanographer *n.*, a scientist who studies oceans and marine life

pollutant *n.*, a substance that makes the environment and water dirty

suffocate *v.*, to die from lack of oxygen

toxic *adj.*, poisonous

urbanization *n.*, the growth of large cities

gorge

bacteria

pollutant

oceanographer

delta

INDEX

SKILLS